WHERE TRUE LOVE IS
DISCUSSION GUIDE

Optimized for use with the Second Edition

A Workbook for Discussion Group Leaders

SUZANNE DEWITT HALL

DH Strategies

Rev. 2.0

ISBN-13: 978-0986408045
ISBN-10: 0986408042

Printed in the United States of America

CONTENTS

Introduction 1

Preparing for your Study 3

    Tips and Tricks 4

    Suggested Kickoff Meeting Format 5

    Suggested Weekly Meeting Format 6

Discussion Materials 7

Concluding Your Study 64

    Suggested Wrap-up Meeting Format 64

Where to Go Next 65

For Further Study 66

INTRODUCTION

> ## "THE TRUTH IS LIKE A LION; YOU DON'T HAVE TO DEFEND IT.
>
> ## LET IT LOOSE; IT WILL DEFEND ITSELF."
>
> (COMMONLY ATTRIBUTED TO ST. AUGUSTINE)

Thank you for your willingness to lead a group through *Where True Love Is*, and to explore what God wants to reveal through the devotional. As the leader, your job is to prepare sacred space in which God's truth freely roams; a space where the Holy Spirit can speak new revelation into the hearts and minds of attendees.

Please understand that it's not your role to argue, convince, or be some sort of truth warrior. You are called simply to this:

To be a conduit which helps clear the way for the Holy Spirit to speak.

Truth is a lion is because Jesus is Truth. Permit the Lion of Love to take charge of each meeting, and ask the Spirit to fall over the group, bringing peace, unity, and joy to your discussions.

My spouse and I are in prayer for you and for your group's work together.

PREPARING FOR YOUR STUDY

HOW TO USE THIS BOOK

The first part of this guide will help you plan:

- Details like whether or not to serve snacks, how to manage time, and what supplies to have on hand.

- The group's kickoff meeting.

- How each weekly session will be structured.

The second part of the guide is a collection of worksheets for use during weekly meetings:

- **Topic Summaries** for you to present as a distillation of the session's overall focus.

- **Daily Summaries** which do the same thing for each daily reading included in the study session. Space is provided after each summary so you can jot down your own thoughts as you read the devotions.

- **Points for Discussion** pages containing questions for participants, which can be photocopied and distributed to study group members.

The guide concludes with a suggested format and questions for your final meeting.

TIPS AND TRICKS

SNACKS!

A hallmark of Jesus' ministry and the early church were people gathering around the table to hear the good news and break bread together. The act of feeding and receiving nourishment leads to connectedness. Consider having a simple snack at each meeting, along with cups and a pitcher of water. Ask participants about food allergies, and plan accordingly. When you've provided a snack for a few weeks, others are likely to offer to bring in a goody, which further helps people draw together because they are contributing to the feeding of both body and soul. If you do choose to include food in your study sessions, be sure to say yes to these offers.

TIME MANAGEMENT

Your goal as facilitator is to encourage discussion, to draw out the quiet people in the group, and to charitably move the conversation out of the hands of over-sharers. But managing time can be a challenge, so here are a few tips:

- Although your study will have start and end times, keep in mind that the group will probably need at least five minutes to settle in and allow for everyone to arrive.

- As you reach the halfway point in the discussion questions, start keeping your eye on the clock. You may need to move things along more quickly in order to finish up on schedule.

- If you aren't great at time keeping, one of the participants may be. Let the group know you're committed to respecting their time, and that you'd appreciate help in paying attention to the clock.

- Alarms or timers on phones are useful. You can set one for 15 minutes before the end, and for 5 minutes before. Since alarms are impersonal, participants' feelings aren't hurt by nudges about needing to move forward.

SUPPLIES

- Each week you'll distribute the discussion questions for the following week, however, be sure to have extra copies on the day of the meeting in case people forget to bring them.

- Have a few Bibles on hand for participants who want to refer to one during your time together.

- For snacks and drinks, plan on having a supply of small plates, napkins, utensils, cups, etc.

SUGGESTED KICKOFF MEETING FORMAT

Here's a suggested outline for your initial meeting.

1. Welcome participants and introduce yourself.

2. Cover logistics such as the location of bathrooms and other pertinent details.

3. Open with prayer.

4. Explain why you are holding this study. Offer a bit of your story as it relates to LGBTQIA+ inclusion and affirmation within the church.

5. Ask participants to introduce themselves and state why they decided to attend the study.

6. Ask the following questions and make note of the answers. You will discuss them again at the conclusion of the study, to see how responses have changed.

   - What are you biggest fears concerning LGBTQIA+ people and faith?
   - What are your concerns for the universal church over this matter?
   - How about your local church?
   - Do you feel equipped to discuss this issue with friends, family, or members of your congregation?

7. Explain the format of the study, and offer guidelines about how you want things to work if you have any (speaking by mutual invitation, method for managing time, etc.)

8. Hand out the first week's discussion questions.

9. Suggest that participants pray before they do each day's reading; that God would reveal what they want them to focus on and how to respond.

10. Let participants know there are no right answers to the questions. Instead, they are meant to encourage thought to help fuel discussion.

11. Distribute a schedule of meeting dates, pointing out any weeks which need to be skipped due to holidays or other events.

12. Let attendees know how long each meeting will last (one and a half hours is recommended).

13. Ask if there are any questions.

14. Close in prayer.

Suggested Weekly Meeting Format

You're obviously free to run your book study any way you'd like, but here's a structure you might find helpful.

1. Open with prayer.

2. Present a high-level summary of the week's readings. (Weekly summaries are provided in this guide.)

3. Invite participants to offer reactions or revelations about the week as a whole.

4. Offer a summary of the first day's reading. (Daily summaries are also provided in this guide.)

5. Go through the first day's discussion questions, inviting participants to share their thoughts.

6. Repeat steps 4 and 5 for the remaining days.

7. Ask for concluding comments or questions.

8. Distribute the following week's discussion questions.

9. Close with prayer.

DISCUSSION MATERIALS

The pages which follow are pairs of materials for each topic area in the study:

- The first pages of each pair are an outline of the topic and the individual days within it. Use this sheet to make notes, and to use as an introduction for topics during group meetings.

- The next pages of each pair are the discussion questions which you can photocopy and distribute to group participants for the following week.

Who is God?

Topic Summary

The study begins with an evaluation of who God *is*, because every other question of faith hinges on that essential truth. The week's readings covered the idea that God is love, a parent and giver of good gifts, the light of the world, server of breakfast, like us in every respect, our judge, and bearer of a holy name.

Daily Summaries

Day 1: Love (1 John 4: 7-8)

The scripture of the day centers around the closing words "God is love." The idea of what unconditional love means was discussed, as was the title of the devotional.

Day 2: Parent and Giver of Good Gifts (Matthew 7:9-11)

The scripture passage describes Jesus saying that God is the giver of good gifts who cares not just about our daily bread, but also about our needs for affirmation and belonging.

Day 3: Light of the World (John 8:12-19)

The John 8 passage talks about Jesus being the light of the world, and that knowing Jesus means knowing the Creator.

Day 4: Server of Breakfast (John 21:1-2, 4-12)

In this devotion, Jesus meets the disciples on the beach after his resurrection, and makes them breakfast, which demonstrates the degree of intimate care God wants to show us.

Day 5: Like Us in Every Respect (Hebrews 2:14-18)

In the Hebrews passage we read of Jesus being like us in *all* ways, so he can understand us well enough to be a merciful high priest.

Day 6: Our Judge (John 5:26-29, 45)

The verses from John tell us that Jesus is the one who will do the judging of our lives, and that our accuser will be Moses if our hope is set on him (and the Law) instead of on Christ.

Day 7: Bearer of a Holy Name (Exodus 20:7)

The passage from Exodus 20 warns against taking the Lord's name in vain, and the devotion discusses keeping God's name holy by only claiming it if we are accurately representing the person of Jesus.

POINTS FOR DISCUSSION ON WHO IS GOD?

Day 1: Love (1 John 4: 7-8)

Why did the author choose to start with this topic?

What does "God is Love" mean to you?

Day 2: Parent and Giver of Good Gifts (Matthew 7:9-11)

What do you suppose the disciples thought about this new idea of God as parent?

What are we to make of that idea now?

Day 3: Light of the World (John 8:12-19)

Why is the message that when we see Jesus, we see the Creator so difficult to accept (both then and now)?

What does being "the light of the world" mean?

Day 4: Server of Breakfast (John 21:1-2, 4-12)

What must the disciples have experienced emotionally when they realized Jesus had cooked them breakfast?

Why would God choose to present himself in this act of simple, subservient care after the resurrection?

Day 5: Like Us in Every Respect (Hebrews 2:14-18)

What does being a sibling of Jesus mean for us?

How are people still held in slavery by fear of death?

Day 6: Our Judge (John 5:26-29, 45)

How does this scripture passage connect to the previous day's?

What does it mean to have Moses as the accuser before the Creator?

Day 7: Bearer of a Holy Name (Exodus 20:7)

What ways are there of taking the Lord's name in vain?

What do you think about the C.S. Lewis quote at the end of the passage?

WHAT IS THE BIBLE? (WEEK ONE)

TOPIC SUMMARY

The week's readings examine a variety of characteristics of scripture, including the idea that they are only truly openable by Jesus, that they are capable of giving wisdom, that they are *not* capable of giving us eternal life, that they are living and active, that they can be safely debated, and that some passages are more important than others.

DAILY SUMMARIES

Day 8: Openable Only by Jesus (Revelation 5:1-9)

The passage from Revelation describes the vision John saw of a lamb receiving a scroll, and elders singing a hymn about the lamb being worthy to open it. The devotion posits that Jesus alone can effectively open the meaning of New Testament scripture for us, and that all of the Bible should be filtered through love.

Day 9: Capable of Giving Wisdom (2 Timothy 3:14-17)

2 Timothy 3:14-17 describes the usefulness of scripture and its inspiration from God.

Day 10: Incapable of Providing Eternal Life (John 5:39-40)

In John 5:39-40, Jesus describes people who think they have eternal life through the scriptures rather than through him.

Day 11: Living and Active (Hebrews 4:12)

Hebrews 4:12 calls the word of God living, active, and sharper than a two-edged sword. The devotion discusses what makes things living versus dead.

Day 12: Safely Debatable (Luke 13:10)

Luke 13:10 shows us that scripture requires insight from Jesus.

Day 13: A Collection of Varyingly Important Passages (Revelation 22:7)

The richness of content in various parts of the Bible is discussed, and the messages of Jesus are prioritized.

Day 14: The Revelation of God's Changing Will (Luke 9:28-35)

Luke's story of Jesus transfigured on the mountain top while in conversation with Elijah and Moses is presented, to illustrate that the Law and the Prophets are to be informed by Christ.

POINTS FOR DISCUSSION ON WHAT IS THE BIBLE (WEEK ONE)

Day 8: Openable Only by Jesus (Revelation 5:1-9)

Why does it take one who is worthy (*the* One) to open the scroll?

What does Eugene Peterson's quote mean, about Jesus being the most "entire" context?

Day 9: Capable of Giving Wisdom (2 Timothy 3:14-17)

What does this day's passage from 2 Timothy tell us about scripture?

Look at the conclusion of the passage. To what end does Paul point?

Day 10: Incapable of Providing Eternal Life (John 5:39-40)

Why didn't those ancient religious want to come to Jesus to have life?

Do you see what is described here in the Christian communities with which you interact?

Day 11: Living and Active (Hebrews 4:12)

What do you think it means that the word of God is living and active and sharper than any two-edged sword?

What transforms scripture from living and active into "the dead letter" mentioned in the final quote?

Day 12: Safely Debatable (Luke 13:10)

Have you encountered people who seem afraid to debate scripture? Have you yourself felt that fear?

How do you think Jesus feels about a group of Christians earnestly engaging in peaceful disagreement about interpretation of scripture? Do you think it offends him?

Day 13: A Collection of Varyingly Important Passages (Revelation 22:7)

What might John's instructions for "keeping" the word of prophecy mean?

Given all the different sections, stories, and literature types of the Bible, what do you think makes some passages more important than others?

Day 14: The Revelation of God's Changing Will (Luke 9:28-35)

What do *you* imagine the conversation between Jesus, Elijah, and Moses was like?

Why might God choose to manifest as a cloud around them?

WHAT IS THE BIBLE? (WEEK TWO)

TOPIC SUMMARY

In this section the examination of scripture continued, with a variety of examples of contradictory scriptures, and some closing thoughts about inerrancy and about using the Bible as an icon rather than making it into an idol.

DAILY SUMMARIES

Day 15: Contradictory: Two Creation Accounts (Genesis 1:11-13 and Genesis 2:4-7 NIV)

Many people claim there is no contradiction in scripture, and yet conflicting accounts of events start in the creation stories presented in Genesis 1 and 2.

Day 16: Contradictory: The Puzzle of Cain (Genesis 4:13-17)

Cain's expulsion after murdering his brother raises interesting questions about who he married.

Day 17: Contradictory: Was it God or Satan? (Samuel 24:1-3 and 1 Chronicles 21:1-3)

The ordering of a census was attributed to Satan in a 1 Chronicles account, but to God in the same story in 2 Samuel 24.

Day 18: Contradictory: On the Flight to Egypt (Matthew 2:13-14 and Luke 2:20-24)

The timing of Mary and Joseph's fulfillment of Jewish Law for circumcision seems to contradict their flight from Bethlehem to Egypt.

Day 19: Contradictory: Paul's Damascus Encounter (Acts 9:3-7 and Acts 22:6-9)

Two contradictory accounts of what happened to the witnesses of Paul's encounter with Jesus on the road to Damascus are examined.

Day 20: Written by Errant People (1 Corinthians 7:12, 1 Corinthians 7:25, and 2 Corinthians 11:17)

The issue of inerrancy is discussed, as introduced by three epistle passages in which Paul states that it's he who is speaking, rather than the Holy Spirit.

Day 21: Icon Not Idol (John 1:1 and John 21:25)

The concept of idolatry is examined, and the confusion some people have between the Word of God (Jesus) and the word of God (the scriptures.)

POINTS FOR DISCUSSION ON WHAT IS THE BIBLE? (WEEK TWO)

Day 15: Contradictory: Two Creation Accounts (Genesis 1:11-13 and Genesis 2:4-7 NIV)

Why do people demand that the Bible doesn't contradict itself?

Is fear part of this reaction? If so, what are they afraid of?

Day 16: Contradictory: The Puzzle of Cain (Genesis 4:13-17)

What explanations have you heard for the Cain question?

Why did God choose to protect Cain?

Day 17: Contradictory: Was it God or Satan? (Samuel 24:1-3 and 1 Chronicles 21:1-3)

Do you know people who demand that the Bible is consistent? How might they respond to conflicting passages like these?

What do you think about the quote which goes along with this day's reading?

Day 18: Contradictory: On the Flight to Egypt (Matthew 2:13-14 and Luke 2:20-24)

If the scriptures are controlled by the Holy Spirit, why would God have permitted contradictions such as these to exist?

The Thomas Paine quote mentions the renunciation of reason. Do you think God wants us to renounce our reason when contemplating scripture?

Day 19: Contradictory: Paul's Damascus Encounter (Acts 9:3-7 and Acts 22:6-9)

Why might Luke have recounted the story two different ways? Did Paul have it wrong?

The quote from Pope Benedict XVI says we are to read scripture as a conversation with God. What is the difference between merely reading something and discussing it with someone?

Day 20: Written by Errant People (1 Corinthians 7:12, 1 Corinthians 7:25, and 2 Corinthians 11:17)

What have you been taught about the inerrancy of scripture?

What do you think about that concept today?

Day 21: Icon Not Idol (John 1:1 and John 21:25)

Have you had experiences with people who seem to believe the Bible *is* God?

The Gregory of Nyssa quote says that people kill each other over idols, and that we need wonder to act as a restorative. How can we apply this restorative?

Jesus as Lawbreaker

Topic Summary

This topic area looked at a few examples of Jesus doing things which went against Jewish Law.

Daily Summaries

Day 22: God Broke the Law by Begetting Jesus (Deuteronomy 22:23-24)

The Deuteronomy 22 prohibition about sexual relations with betrothed women was introduced, and contrasted with the story of the Holy Spirit's coming upon Mary when she conceived Jesus.

Day 23: Jesus Broke the Sabbath Repeatedly (John 5:16-18)

The first example of Jesus' violation of the Sabbath is offered, in a story from John 5 in which some religious experts sought to kill him.

Day 24: Jesus Defends Breaking the Sabbath (Mark 2:23-27)

In this story, Jesus defends his disciples traveling on the Sabbath and picking grain, both of which were prohibited activities.

Day 25: Pharisees Seek Jesus' Death Due to His Violations (Mark 3:1-6)

This day's reading shows another violation of the Sabbath, when Jesus heals a man's withered hand and a group of Pharisees plotted to kill him because of the violation of Law.

Day 26: Jesus Suggests Violating a Commandment (Matthew 8:18-22)

In the Matthew passage, Jesus suggests that a follower should break one of the Ten Commandments by ignoring the obligation to bury his father.

Day 27: Jesus Violates Purification Laws (Mark 5:25-34)

Jesus is touched by an "unclean" woman who had an issue of blood for 12 years, and doesn't fulfill the Law's requirements for ritual purification.

Day 28: Jesus Commands the Consumption of Blood (John 6:53-61)

One of the most important Laws in the Hebrew Scriptures—a prohibition against consuming the blood of animals—is turned on its head by Jesus' command to eat his flesh and drink his blood.

POINTS FOR DISCUSSION ON JESUS AS LAWBREAKER

Day 22: God Broke the Law by Begetting Jesus (Deuteronomy 22:23-24)

What must it have been like for Mary to agree to conceive Jesus by the Holy Spirit, knowing she had already entered into the multi-stage marital contract with Joseph?

The quote for the day says that love is never constrained, and always seeks to do more than what is asked of it. Mary's yes is self-donating in that way; knowing that she could face hardships for agreeing to be impregnated by someone other than her husband. Her yes was an agreement to self-donation potentially even to the point of death. What does this tell us about God's hope for our own responses to their requests for scandalous actions of love?

Day 23: Jesus Broke the Sabbath Repeatedly (John 5:16-18)

Why do you think Jesus would repeatedly break Sabbath rules, despite their importance in the Ten Commandments, the Law, and throughout the Old Testament stories?

What are the hallmarks of the religion Jesus demonstrated versus a rule-driven ethical system of faith?

Day 24: Jesus Defends Breaking the Sabbath (Mark 2:23-27)

What should Jesus' determination that care for human hunger overrides the Law tell us about God's priorities?

What are your thoughts about the Thomas Jefferson quote at the end of the reading? Does it surprise you?

Day 25: Pharisees Seek Jesus' Death Due to His Violations (Mark 3:1-6)

Do hardened Christian hearts continue to grieve Jesus today? If yes, how?

Jesus doesn't pause to consider whether he should heal the withered hand of the man in this story. Do you think he would do the same for withered hearts today?

Day 26: Jesus Suggests Violating a Commandment (Matthew 8:18-22)

How important is it for most people to attend to the burial of a parent?

What is Jesus suggesting the disciples choose over the commanded obligation of parental respect?

Day 27: Jesus Violates Purification Laws (Mark 5:25-34)

The woman with the issue of blood was considered unclean. LGBTQIA+ people are viewed by some fundamentalist Christians as unclean. Would it be okay with God if people tried to stop her (or them) from reaching for Jesus' hem?

What sort of an evangelist must this woman have become after this experience? What kind of evangelists might LGBTQIA+ people who are embraced by churches today become?

Is there some hidden issue or fear you need to approach Jesus about in the same way? (This question is for contemplation only. No need to share your answer with the group.)

Day 28: Jesus Commands the Consumption of Blood (John 6:53-61)

The disciples struggled to understand how Jesus could be a man of God given that he commanded something which was such a violation of Law. Jesus' message was so shocking that many disciples stopped following him. Why has much of Christianity become so bland and tame in comparison to Jesus' message and actions of radically inclusive love?

What must the blessing have been like for the disciples who stayed despite being shocked? What might the blessing be like for those today who try to love and include radically as Jesus did?

Law as Problematic

Topic Summary

This topic area examined scriptures which describe problems related to the Law along with Jesus' words about those problems.

Daily Summaries

Day 29: The Letter Kills (2 Corinthians 3:5-6)

In his second letter to the Corinthians, Paul describes our sufficiency as coming from Jesus Christ, and states that the letter kills.

Day 30: Perfection Cannot be Achieved through Law (Hebrews 7:11-14, 18-22)

The Hebrews passage summarizes the problems of the Law, calling them weak, useless, and able to make nothing perfect, which is why Jesus came as a new priest who is guarantor of a better covenant.

Day 31: Jesus Points Out Flaws in the Law (Numbers 30:1-2 and Matthew 5:33-37)

This day's devotional examines Jesus' correction of the old Law related to vows.

Day 32: The Law Is a Shadow (Hebrews 8:3, 5-7)

The verses in Hebrews point out that the old ways of doing things—with all the Laws about sacrifices and tabernacles—were merely a shadow of the new covenant offered through Jesus.

Day 33: Law Creates Unholy Zeal (Romans 10:1-4)

The devotion highlights the problem of pride in not submitting to the new commandments of Jesus and discusses Paul's prayer that the Israelites would seek Christ's righteousness rather than striving to follow Law.

Day 34: Law is Too Heavy to Carry (Luke 11:45-51)

Luke describes Jesus admonishing the experts in the Law for heaping burdens too heavy to bear on those who strive to love and serve God.

Day 35: Law Creates Judgment Based on Appearances (John 7:11-24)

The scripture recounts another of Jesus' encounters with some Jewish leaders. This time he tells them they need to judge "correctly" rather than by a strict adherence to Law.

POINTS FOR DISCUSSION ON LAW AS PROBLEMATIC

Day 29: The Letter Kills (2 Corinthians 3:5-6)

What does it look like to be a minister of the life-giving Spirit?

What is the perfection manifested which Thomas Merton mentions in the final quote?

Day 30: Perfection Cannot be Achieved through Law (Hebrews 7:11-14, 18-22)

Do you ever struggle with striving for perfection according to your own set of Christian rules and regulations?

The author of Hebrews says the Law makes nothing perfect, yet many Christians demand that LGBTQIA+ people can only be Christian if they deny the reality of their authentic selves. Why are gender and sexual identity such an area of focus when they are mentioned so seldom in the Bible in comparison to issues like pride and lack of charity?

Day 31: Jesus Points Out Flaws in the Law (Numbers 30:1-2 and Matthew 5:33-37)

What do you think about the final sentence of the Eric Metaxas quote? What is deeper than religious legalism?

John 21:25 tells us the world isn't big enough to hold all the books needed to describe the things Jesus did. What is the likelihood therefore that Jesus did and said even more things to illustrate that the old Law was problematic?

Day 32: The Law Is a Shadow (Hebrews 8:3, 5-7)

Why are so many Christians fearful of admitting that the old covenant Laws had faults, when today's Hebrews passage is pretty clear that they did?

How do we regulate all of life by the eternal Law of the one who is Love, as Gandhi's quote suggests?

Day 33: Law Creates Unholy Zeal (Romans 10:1-4)

What should the impact on our faith be of Paul saying "Christ is the culmination of the law so that there may be righteousness for everyone who believes."?

What does zeal based on love rather than Law look like?

Day 34: Law is Too Heavy to Carry (Luke 11:45-51)

How heavy a burden do you think LGBTQIA+ young people carry when the religious experts in their churches load them down with Law-driven proclamations of hell?

How can we manifest the moral courage Robert F. Kennedy's quote mentions in light of the LGBTQIA+ exclusion that is prevalent in so many denominations?

Day 35: Law Creates Judgment Based on Appearances (John 7:11-24)

Jesus urged those who questioned him to stop judging by appearances, but instead to judge correctly. What does judging correctly look like?

Have you ever been called a deceiver or demonically influenced based on your defense of LGBTQIA+ inclusion and affirmation? How did you handle it? Would you handle it differently now?

JESUS AS FULFILLMENT OF THE LAW

TOPIC SUMMARY

Many people who use the Bible as a basis for excluding LGBTQIA+ folks repeat Jesus' words about his coming not to abolish but to fulfill the law. In doing so, they miss the key reality that he has *done* the fulfilling. The devotional's last section on the Law examines how Jesus fulfills it, through his time on earth and on the cross.

DAILY SUMMARIES

Day 36: Jesus' Commandments Trump All Law (Matthew 22:34-40 and Mark 12:28-31)

In the first day's devotion, Jesus offers clarification about which is the first and most important commandment: to love God with our whole hearts, souls, minds, and strength. It also discusses the importance of the word "commandment" in comparison to "instruction" or other terms.

Day 37: This Is the Law and the Prophets (Matthew 7:12)

In the Matthew passage, Jesus says that the Golden Rule is the Law and the Prophets.

Day 38: Jesus Fulfills the Law (Matthew 5:17-18, John 4:34, John 17:4, John 19:28, and John 19:30)

The devotion offers a number of passages which indicate that Jesus' fulfillment/accomplishment of the Law has taken place.

Day 39: Jesus Ransoms Us From the Law (Galatians 4:4-7)

Paul's letter to the Galatians tells us life under the Law was a form of imprisonment and slavery, but in the fulfilling of Jesus' mission, we were transformed from slaves to adopted children and heirs.

Day 40: Love Is the Fulfilling of the Law (Romans 13:8-10)

The day's devotion focuses on Paul's letters once again; this time he points out that loving others and doing no harm is the fulfillment of the Law.

Day 41: Righteousness Comes through Jesus (Galatians 5:4-6)

The Galatians passage explains that when we cling to issues of the Law, we become estranged from Christ.

Day 42: Loving God and Neighbor Is Fulfillment of the Law (Mark 12:32-34 and Luke 10:25-28)

Stories from Mark and Luke are presented in which Jesus points out that loving God and loving our neighbors as ourselves bring us close to the kingdom, and lead to eternal life.

POINTS FOR DISCUSSION ON JESUS AS FULFILLMENT OF THE LAW

Day 36: Jesus' Commandments Trump All Law (Matthew 22:34-40 and Mark 12:28-31)

Given Jesus' use of the word "commandment," how important should we consider these passages for our Christian walk?

Does Jesus' rolling up of all the commandments into these two make life easier as his followers or harder?

Day 37: This Is the Law and the Prophets (Matthew 7:12)

How do you think LGBTQIA+ individuals want people of faith to treat them?

How can you ensure you're doing what Jesus requests in today's reading?

Day 38: Jesus Fulfills the Law (Matthew 5:17-18, John 4:34, John 17:4, John 19:28, and John 19:30)

The concluding quote says that overcoming legalism requires real obedience to Christ. What *is* real obedience to him?

How many letters of the Law are no longer followed by Christians?

Day 39: Jesus Ransoms Us from the Law (Galatians 4:4-7)

Why do we seem so eager to return to slavery or tyranny of Law?

What things might appear in a vision if Jesus were to drop a sheet in today's legalistic churches?

Day 40: Love Is the Fulfilling of the Law (Romans 13:8-10)

John Wesley's quote asks and answers a question: "What religion do I preach? The religion of love." What religion do *you* preach?

How do you fulfill the Law through loving during difficult situations?

Day 41: Righteousness Comes through Jesus (Galatians 5:4-6)

Is the church today still drawn to the idea that righteousness is connected to rules and regulations?

How do we prevent ourselves from becoming "estranged from Christ?"

Day 42: Loving God and Neighbor Is Fulfillment of the Law (Mark 12:32-34 and Luke 10:25-28)

How can we encourage our fellow Christians who *do* embrace the concept that love is most important, as Jesus did for the people in today's verses?

Have you ever encountered a "bait and clobber" Jesus in those who argue for LGBTQIA+ exclusion from church?

CAN A SINNER BE CHRISTIAN?

TOPIC SUMMARY

This topic area dispels the notion that someone cannot be Christian and yet sin.

NOTE: The existence of this topic does not imply LGBTQIA+ sinfulness. The book as a whole is an answer to that question, which the author vehemently believes otherwise. It's included because the idea of Christians not sinning is frequently brought up by non-affirming people of faith. LGBTQIA+ people as a group are neither more nor less sinful than any other group, but the idea of Christian sinlessness nevertheless needs to be dispelled.

DAILY SUMMARIES

Day 43: Jesus Calls His Disciples Evil (Matthew 7: 11)

The Matthew passage is an excerpt from the Sermon on the Mount, when Jesus calls all those listening "evil," including the disciples who were among the crowd.

Day 44: Paul Calls Himself a Sinner (1 Timothy 1:16 and Romans 7:15-25)

In passages from 1 Timothy and Romans, Paul self-describes as being sinful despite having been knocked off his high horse by Christ.

Day 45: Jesus Calls Peter Satan (Matthew 16:16-23)

In this devotion, Jesus speaks to Peter about his passion to come, and Peter rebukes him about it. In response, Jesus says "Get behind me, Satan!"

Day 46: John Tells Us What to do When We Sin (1 John 2:1-2)

In this reading, John writes about trying not to sin, but reassures the young church that when sinning does occur, Jesus will be our advocate.

Day 47: Jesus Praises a Worshipper of Many Gods (Matthew 8:5-11)

The Matthew passage highlights a confession of faith by a polytheistic Roman centurion and Jesus' words of praise in response.

Day 48: Tax Collectors and Prostitutes Enter Heaven (Matthew 21:23, 31-32)

This day's devotion warns the chief priests and elders that tax collectors and prostitutes are entering the kingdom of heaven before them.

Day 49: If We Claim to Be Without Sin We Deceive Ourselves (Romans 3:9-10, 22-25, and 1 John 1:8-10)

In a set of three readings, we are shown not only that followers of Jesus continue to sin, but also that those who deny sinning are deceiving themselves.

POINTS FOR DISCUSSION ON CAN A SINNER BE CHRISTIAN?

Day 43: Jesus Calls His Disciples Evil (Matthew 7: 11)

Do you know anyone who believes "saved" people can no longer sin, and if they do sin, they must not actually be saved? Have you believed this yourself?

The conclusion of the Matthew passage connotes that God gives good things to us even though we are all "evil." How should this inform our own behavior toward others?

Day 44: Paul Calls Himself a Sinner (1 Timothy 1:16 and Romans 7:15-25)

How should Paul's humble admission to Timothy and the church in Rome instruct our own stances when debating faith issues?

What do you think about the last sentence in the concluding Bonhoeffer quote?

Day 45: Jesus Calls Peter Satan (Matthew 16:16-23)

Jesus suffered at the hands of empire and humanity's rejection of a new image of love. LGBTQIA+ people suffer when they go to church knowing that people are judging them as unworthy to be there. What might the blessing be for them in heaven for seeking God despite all the blockades placed in the way of that search?

Jesus didn't require Peter to be sinless in order for him to do mighty work in the church. What does God require of *you* for the mission you were created to fulfill?

Day 46: John Tells Us What to Do When We Sin (1 John 2:1-2)

Jesus is our defense attorney who can explain the circumstances of our sin. What do we offer to him to counter all the negative stuff we do?

What is our calling according to St. Isaac the Syrian in the final quote?

Day 47: Jesus Praises a Worshipper of Many Gods (Matthew 8:5-11)

Jesus was amazed by the faith of a polytheistic Centurion. Do you think God rejects the faith of LGBTQIA+ people?

Is there any way of meriting salvation?

Day 48: Tax Collectors and Prostitutes Enter Heaven (Matthew 21:23, 31-32)

What do you think about the reality that despised people (as exemplified by tax collectors and prostitutes) are entering the kingdom of heaven before religious leaders?

Bonhoeffer suggest that we regard people in light of what they suffer. How do we do that?

Day 49: If We Claim to Be Without Sin We Deceive Ourselves (Romans 3:9-10, 22-25, and 1 John 1:8-10)

Paul and John both felt compelled to offer instructions about the reality of sin in the life of the church. Why then do so many of the faithful deny that Christians commit it?

Rather than searching for distinctions between people in order that we can claim who does and doesn't have access to God, how can we more actively seek to open ourselves and others to be known and loved by God as Nouwen suggests?

Who Does Jesus Condemn and Why?

Topic Summary

Previous topics revealed that Jesus was quite a rebel, and was radically inclusive. However, he did chastise people with some regularity. This topic explored who those people were.

Daily Summaries

Day 50: Those Who Shut the Door of Heaven (Matthew 23:13, 35)

In this reading, Jesus calls a group of Pharisees and teachers of the Law hypocrites who shut the door of heaven in people's faces.

Day 51: Neglectors of Justice, Mercy, and Faith (Matthew 23:23-24)

Jesus' outrage continues in the Matthew passage, when he describes legalists who focus on tiny bits of Law while neglecting the weightier matters of mercy and justice.

Day 52: Prophet Killers (Matthew 23:33-34)

Jesus continues his sermon of woes by calling the religious leaders snakes and a brood of vipers who aren't willing to listen to the voices of the prophets.

Day 53: Blind Pharisees (John 9:39-41)

In this devotion, John describes Jesus calling some Pharisees' claims of clear-sighted views on Law "blindness."

Day 54: Prideful Pharisees (Luke 18:9-14)

The passage describes Jesus telling Pharisees who were convinced of their righteousness and looked down on others a parable about a humble tax collector being justified before a prideful Pharisee.

Day 55: Deniers of Access to God (John 2:13-17)

John tells a story of Jesus' anger at those who controlled access to God's temple and prevented others from entering.

Day 56: Those Who Will Not Produce Good Fruit (Matthew 3:7-10 and Galatians 5:22-23)

In this devotion, the expectation that Christians produce good fruit is explored.

Points for Discussion on Who Does Jesus Condemn and Why?

Day 50: Those Who Shut the Door of Heaven (Matthew 23:13, 35)

Jesus described a door of heaven. The closing quote mentions a line with people on either side. On which side do you see yourself in these images?

How do we open doors to the heaven rather than shutting them in people's faces?

Day 51: Neglectors of Justice, Mercy, and Faith (Matthew 23:23-24)

What are modern day examples of straining out a gnat and swallowing a camel?

How do we focus on the weightier matters of the Law: justice, mercy, and faith?

Day 52: Prophet Killers (Matthew 23:33-34)

Can you identify any prophets in your own life?

Are there things you regret saying or doing in the past to a prophet who tried to speak truth to you?

Day 53: Blind Pharisees (John 9:39-41)

What is Jesus telling us about the "sin of certainty?"

What is the true vision Jesus describes and how do we incorporate it into our lives and the lives of our churches?

Day 54: Prideful Pharisees (Luke 18:9-14)

How do we prevent ourselves from feeling superior and more righteous than others?

How do we change our ideas of a "dreamed of Christian Community" to match God's?

Day 55: Deniers of Access to God (John 2:13-17)

What is the impact on someone when they have to hide who they are in order to go to church?

How would your experience of church change if you realized you didn't have anything to hide?

Day 56: Those Who Will Not Produce Good Fruit (Matthew 3:7-10 and Galatians 5:22-23)

Does a demand for strict adherence to Law by legalistic Christians tend to coincide with the production of the fruit of the Spirit?

Are you producing fruit? (No need to answer for the group. Just evaluate for yourself.) If not, why not?

What Does Jesus Ask Us to Do?

Topic Summary

Until this point, the book has focused on things Jesus warns against, but all that shifts starting with this section. Devotions in this topic area focus on statements Jesus made about what God wants from us.

Daily Summaries

Day 57: Worship in Spirit and Truth (John 4:19-24)

In this reading we see that Jesus doesn't ask that rules and regulations be adhered to in order for us to be his followers. Instead, he counsels worshipping in spirit and truth.

Day 58: Seek Unity (John 17:20-26)

The passage from John 17 recounts Jesus' prayer that his followers be one as the Trinity is one, so that the world might see and believe.

Day 59: Do Justice (Isaiah 58:6-9)

In this devotion, we looked back at the words of the prophet Isaiah to see that God desires us "to loose the bonds of injustice, to undo the thongs of the yoke, to let the oppressed go free, and to break every yoke? Is it not to share your bread with the hungry, and bring the homeless poor into your house."

Day 60: Wash Feet (Luke7:36-39)

Luke 7 tells the story of a sinful woman who comes to the house where Jesus is dining and washes his feet with her tears, wipes them with her hair, and anoints them with expensive perfume, much to the dismay of his self-righteous host.

Day 61: Be Like Children (Matthew 18:1-4)

The devotion describes Jesus saying that people who are as humble as little children will be exalted in heaven.

Day 62: Keep His Commandments (John 14:15, 23-24)

John 14 reminds us that when we love Jesus, we honor, keep, and do the things he commands of us (which are to love God with our whole mind, heart, soul, and strength, and to love others as ourselves.)

Day 63: Love Yourself (Matthew 22:37-39)

This devotion focuses on the last part of the greatest commandment, when we are instructed to love ourselves.

POINTS FOR DISCUSSION ON WHAT DOES JESUS ASK US TO DO?

Day 57: Worship in Spirit and Truth (John 4:19-24)

What is your experience of worshipping in the Spirit?

Where do you experience God most profoundly?

Day 58: Seek Unity (John 17:20-26)

What does it mean in John 17:26 that the love with which the Creator loved Jesus would be in us, and Jesus in us?

What sort of supporting role are you playing in the lives of the LGBTQIA+ people you know?

Day 59: Do Justice (Isaiah 58:6-9)

Can the world see the Christ in you shining through actions of social justice as Isaiah outlines?

What does Isaiah tell us the reward will be if we break every yoke, remove the accusing finger, and free the oppressed?

Day 60: Wash Feet (Luke 7:36-39)

The story of the sinful woman washing Jesus' feet leads him to wash the feet of the disciples, even those of Judas. There is a mutuality of receiving and passing on. How do we live into this model of service and reception?

What humble acts of kindness do you offer others? What humble acts of kindness do you receive?

Day 61: Be Like Children (Matthew 18:1-4)

What does being childlike in approaching God mean to you?

How can LGBTQIA+ people speak optimistically of sunshine despite the storm clouds of exclusion?

Day 62: Keep His Commandments (John 14:15, 23-24)

How do we live with Jesus as our new commandment?

Jesus points out numerous times that when we see and hear him we see and hear the Creator. Do you feel different emotional responses to God as described in the Old Testament in comparison to Jesus?

Day 63: Love Yourself (Matthew 22:37-39)

Do you love God with your whole heart? What gets in the way of that?

Do you find it hard to love yourself? What gets in the way of your self-acceptance and love?

MALE AND FEMALE, GOD CREATED THEM

TOPIC SUMMARY

This topic explores the issue of gender from the context of scripture.

DAILY SUMMARIES

Day 64: Male AND Female God Created Them (Genesis 1:26-27)

The first of two accounts of human creation was reviewed with a focus on the phrase "in the image of God he created them; male *and* female God created them."

Day 65: The Complexity of Biological Sex (Matthew 19:4)

The issue of male *and* female is explored through the lens of genetics.

Day 66: Prisoners of our Bodies (Acts 12:6-11)

In this devotion, the story of Peter being freed from prison by an angel is used to frame the idea that people who believe they are a gender other than that which society expects of them can feel like prisoners of their own bodies.

Day 67: Like Us in All Ways (Hebrews 2:14-17)

Hebrews 2 talks about how Jesus—our high-priest advocate and our judge—is like us in *all* ways.

Day 68: Fearfully and Wonderfully Made (Psalm 139:7-16)

Psalm 139 beautifully unfolds the mystery of our being formed in our mothers' wombs, and that there is no hiding from God.

Day 69: The Subtle Shifting of Gender (Genesis 9:14-15)

This devotion features God's promise to Noah in the form of a rainbow, with hues that shift invisibly from one into the next.

Day 70: Gender Identification in the Talmud (Genesis 5:1-2)

A final look at the "male and female, God created them" concept is offered, along with a peek at non-binary gender definitions in the Talmud.

POINTS FOR DISCUSSION ON MALE AND FEMALE, GOD CREATED THEM

Day 64: Male AND Female God Created Them (Genesis 1:26-27)

Do you have trouble thinking about God as being something other than masculine?

What is your emotional response to the idea that God is male *and* female?

Day 65: The Complexity of Biological Sex (Matthew 19:4)

What is the perceived value or importance of demanding binaries in sexuality, biological sex, and gender? What is the driving force which fuels the arguments against non-binary understandings?

Human protective tendencies make us want to shun differentness, when those very differences reflect particular characteristics of God's beauty. Is it possible for us to outgrow or evolve away from those tendencies?

Day 66: Prisoners of our Bodies (Acts 12:6-11)

Are you in any prisons right now?

How can you be attuned to others who are spiritually or emotionally imprisoned so that you can be an angelic voice inviting freedom?

Day 67: Like Us in All Ways (Hebrews 2:14-17)

Is it hard for you to imagine Jesus as having the depth and breadth of understanding and compassion described in today's reading?

Do you see yourself as a living, breathing, priceless work of art?

Day 68: Fearfully and Wonderfully Made (Psalm 139:7-16)

Have you ever tried to hide from God?

Why do so many of us condemn others for the divinely added unique bits in the genetics provided by their mothers and fathers? What are those things in you?

Day 69: The Subtle Shifting of Gender (Genesis 9:14-15)

Why do we fight so hard to be some other color than we are, or to force others to change their colors?

How much more magnificent is it to see yourself as a living, breathing part of a spectrum of color rather than merely black or white? Which is a better reflection of the image of God?

Day 70: Gender Identification in the Talmud (Genesis 5:1-2)

For what purpose does God invent each of us to be unique?

What would the world be like if this wasn't the case?

Sexuality and Marriage (Week One)

Topic Summary

In the first week of this topic area, an initial exploration of marriage in the scriptures is offered.

Daily Summaries

Day 71: The Sacredness of Sexuality (Jeremiah 20:7, 9)

Passages from Jeremiah 20 convey the passionate desire for union with the beloved.

Day 72: Sex Outside of Marriage (Song of Songs 4:9-16)

The concept of disordered versus godly marital relationships is introduced through a passage from the Bible's great love poem attributed to Solomon.

Day 73: Adam and Eve are NOT the Optimal Model for Marriage (Genesis 2:18, 21-22)

In this devotion, the creation of Eve from Adam's bit of flesh is explored to determine whether the first couple is a good example for marriage.

Day 74: "Traditional" Marriage (1 Timothy 3:1-6)

The 1 Timothy 3 passage shows us that the one-man/multiple women form of marriage was still in play in early Christianity. The practice continued for generations after that, which means that polygyny is really "traditional marriage."

Day 75: What God Has Joined Together (Mark 10:2-9)

A group of Pharisees tried to trick Jesus with questions about divorce, which led to his response that when God draws a couple together, no one should try to separate them. But the author poses the question: are all marriages ordained by God?

Day 76: One Man, One Woman, Many Slaves (Ephesians 6:5-9)

Ephesians 5 is often used as an enduring demand that marriage should be between one man and one woman. But the instructions about slavery which come just a few verses later in Ephesians 6 are cast off as historical relics.

Day 77: Let Marriage be Held in Honor (Hebrews 13:4)

Hebrews 13 urges readers to hold marriage in honor, and the author raises a few examples of marriages to see which model is more honoring of God's desire for the institution.

POINTS FOR DISCUSSION ON SEXUALITY AND MARRIAGE (WEEK ONE)

Day 71: The Sacredness of Sexuality (Jeremiah 20:7, 9)

Do you find it hard to view sexuality as sacred? If yes, why?

How might our sexuality be a reflection of God?

Day 72: Sex Outside of Marriage (Song of Songs 4:9-16)

The Song of Songs is a unique book; a conversation between lovers in poem form. Why do you think it's included in Hebrew Scriptures?

How might sexual intimacy change if we invite God into each act?

Day 73: Adam and Eve are NOT the Optimal Model for Marriage (Genesis 2:18, 21-22)

What is marriage supposed to be about?

What are the characteristics of a marriage which God desires?

Day 74: "Traditional" Marriage (1 Timothy 3:1-6)

Did this reading change your view of "traditional marriage" at all?

How can your approach to marriage contribute to the way future generations view what "traditional marriage" means?

Day 75: What God Has Joined Together (Mark 10:2-9)

Do you know people who seem to be in marriages ordained by God? Do you know others who pretty clearly are *not*?

How does a couple discern whether God has brought them together?

Day 76: One Man, One Woman, Many Slaves (Ephesians 6:5-9)

Why do socially conservative Christians find it so easy to dismiss instructions about slavery but demand the marriage instructions a few verses earlier be followed to the letter?

The closing quote says that same-sex couples may be the institution of marriage's best friend. How does having to fight to be married impact its perceived value?

Day 77: Let Marriage be Held in Honor (Hebrews 13:4)

Adultery is rampant in our culture. The importance of fidelity is stressed throughout the scriptures, and summarized in this Hebrews passage. Why isn't there widespread condemnation of adultery rather than of covenantal same-sex relationships?

Marriage doesn't seem to be very highly respected any more. How do we hold all marriage in honor?

SEXUALITY AND MARRIAGE (WEEK TWO)

TOPIC SUMMARY

Sexuality and marriage continue to be discussed, along with passages about Sodom and Gomorrah.

DAILY SUMMARIES

Day 78: Marriage as a Rule of Love (Ephesians 5:22-23, 31-32)

This devotion unpacks Paul's instructions to the Ephesians about a woman's allegiance once she is married, then moves on to his urging men toward love.

Day 79: Even Their Women Exchanged Natural Sexual Relations (Romans 1:26-27)

The Romans verses describe some of the things which occurred in idolatrous communities in days past, and warn against lust and uncontrolled passions.

Day 80: The Wisest Man Had Hundreds of Wives (1 Kings 10:23-24, and 11:1-4, 9)

In 1 Kings 10 and 11 we read about Solomon's many loves, and how his attention turned to other gods. But nowhere did we see God angry about the wives and concubines themselves.

Day 81: The False Understanding of Sodom and Gomorrah (Genesis 19:1-5)

This devotion opens several days of readings about the destruction of Sodom and Gomorrah. In this case, the author asks if the issue was about sex rather than rape, why the men of the town didn't simply turn to each other to satisfy their lust.

Day 82: Lot's Daughters Are Offered Up (Genesis 19:6-8)

Genesis 19:6-8 describes Lot offering his virgin daughters to the angry horde.

Day 83: Lot's Daughters Commit Incest (Genesis 19:30-36)

This devotion looks at what happens after the cities are destroyed, Lot's wife has been transformed into a pillar of salt, and Lot and his daughters have fled to the mountains. A tale of incestuous rape follows.

Day 84: Isaiah and Ezekiel on Sodom and Gomorrah (Isaiah 1:10-11, 13, 15-20 and Ezekiel 16:49)

While many socially conservative Christians claim that the Sodom and Gomorrah story is all about God's anger at homosexual behavior, Isaiah and Ezekiel report otherwise.

Points for Discussion on Sexuality and Marriage (Week Two)

Day 78: Marriage as a Rule of Love (Ephesians 5:22-23, 31-32)

Do you think the kind of marriage Paul describes is still a "great secret?"

What is the essence of becoming one flesh with a spouse?

Day 79: Even Their Women Exchanged Natural Sexual Relations (Romans 1:26-27)

Why is lust problematic?

How do we ensure that sex doesn't become our god, but instead draw God into sex?

Day 80: The Wisest Man Had Hundreds of Wives (1 Kings 10:23-24, and 11:1-4, 9)

The wisest man in the Bible was not able to lead by example in the area of fidelity to God. What should that tell us about our own struggles to be faithful?

If God was not angry at Solomon (or at the numerous other polygynous faith heroes) for not following the one man/one woman model of marriage, why would God be mad at modern-day Christ-centered unions which similarly don't follow it?

Day 81: The False Understanding of Sodom and Gomorrah (Genesis 19:1-5)

The good news which entered Sodom in the form of angels incited the locals into a frenzied lynch mob. Could people who vehemently oppose same-sex marriage be reacting to the light manifested by Christ-centered same-sex couples?

Day 82: Lot's Daughters Are Offered Up (Genesis 19:6-8)

If the Sodom and Gomorrah story is about homosexuals, why would Lot offer females as a substitute? Gay men would not be interested in Lot's daughters.

Why were the guests who sheltered under Lot's roof more deserving of protection than the Lot's daughters?

Day 83: Lot's Daughters Commit Incest (Genesis 19:30-36)

What is your reaction to this story?

The act of incestuous rape by Lot's daughters was both sinful and showed a lack of faith in God's provision. Why weren't *they* killed or turned into pillars of salt?

Day 84: Isaiah and Ezekiel on Sodom and Gomorrah (Isaiah 1:10-11, 13, 15-20 and Ezekiel 16:49)

Misattribution of the destruction of Sodom and Gomorrah as due to sexual sinfulness apparently started early, because God called on the Major Prophets to clarify the problem. What does God say to us through Isaiah and Ezekiel about the cause of God's anger?

How should God's expectation for doing right and seeking justice reflect out to the LGBTQIA+ community?

What Does it Take to Get to Heaven?

Topic Summary

The final week of devotions looks at what it takes to be saved.

Daily Summaries

Day 85: For God so Loved the World (John 3:16)

The famous words from John 3:16 are unpacked: that whoever believes in Jesus is not condemned.

Day 86: Not Everyone Who Says Lord, Lord… (Matthew 7:21-23)

The warning Jesus issued in Matthew 7:21-23 comes at the end of a long list of instructions about the behavior he wants from his followers, including good works, offering forgiveness, loving neighbors, trusting in God's provision, not showing off your piety, not judging, doing unto others, etc.

Day 87: Evaluation by the Just Judge (John 5:25-30)

John 5 describes the final judgement, when Jesus will conduct an examination of our lives and use *his* assessment to determine the outcome.

Day 88: Sheep and Goats (Matthew 25:31-36, 40-43, 45-46)

Jesus' description of the last judgement continues the theme, with a look at how God will judge sheep from goats based on how people are cared for or mistreated.

Day 89: Righteousness Through Faith (Romans 4:13-15, 18, 22)

In this devotion, Paul talks about the righteousness that came through faith rather than Law in Abraham's story, and how Jesus returns us to that state of simplicity.

Day 90: Whoever Calls on the Name of the Lord Shall Be Saved (Romans 10:11-13)

In the final day of reading, we hear Paul's reminder that whoever calls upon the name of the Lord shall be saved.

Conclusion: (1 Corinthians 13:12)

The study closes with a beautiful vision of what takes place when our physical bodies die and the barriers to oneness with God and creation are removed.

POINTS FOR DISCUSSION ON WHAT DOES IT TAKE TO GET TO HEAVEN?

Day 85: For God so Loved the World (John 3:16)

Why do so many Christians sweep aside the powerfully inclusive statements by the beloved disciple, that whoever believes in Jesus is not condemned?

What do you think about the last line of the A.W. Tozer quote?

Day 86: Not Everyone Who Says Lord, Lord... (Matthew 7:21-23)

How do we find our own way of following Jesus without creating boxes of rules and exclusivity?

How do you focus on and listen to the gleam of heaven which is already inside you?

Day 87: Evaluation by the Just Judge (John 5:25-30)

How do you respond to the idea of Jesus as judge compared to the Old Testament depiction of God as judge?

Why do we set ourselves up to be judges who exclude LGBTQIA+ people and deny them the right to marriage, ordination, and full participation in the life of the church?

Day 88: Sheep and Goats (Matthew 25:31-36, 40-43, 45-46)

Why isn't this passage given more attention by modern-day religious Law-wielders?

What do you want Jesus to report about you on the "evening of your life?"

Day 89: Righteousness Through Faith (Romans 4:13-15, 18, 22)

The salvation story begins (through Abraham) and ends (through Jesus) with a simple model of righteousness based on faith. How can we avoid becoming embroiled in a muddled, Law-based view of earned righteousness?

How do we live in a way which illustrates that there is nothing higher or greater than love?

Day 90: Whoever Calls on the Name of the Lord Shall be Saved (Romans 10:11-13)

Jewish members of the early church were fearful of intermixing with non-Jews. Might today's legalistic Christians have some fear of mixing with LGBTQIA+ people in the church?

How do we overcome the religious pride which tries to shame others when they simply want to be part of the church?

Conclusion: (1 Corinthians 13:12)

What are your thoughts about the author's description of the afterlife?

How important will sexual or gender identity be in this vision?

Concluding Your Study

Suggested Wrap-up Meeting Format

You've worked your way through *Where True Love Is*, gotten to know each other a whole lot better as a group, and hopefully explored scripture in a way you haven't before. All of these things are worthy of celebration! If it fits your style, consider holding a potluck at the final meeting, so everyone can let their hair down a bit, break bread together, and share their conclusions about the study.

Here's an outline for how you might want to run this last get together.

1. Gather, pray, and eat (if you do decide to hold a potluck). Participating in your discussion group will have built community between members. While eating, people can simply enjoy each other's company and chat.

2. As dessert is served, ask for thoughts about the overall experience of the study.

3. Once that is complete, remind participants of the questions you asked at the kickoff meeting, and announce that it's time to run through them again:

   - What are you biggest fears concerning LGBTQIA+ people and faith?

   - What are your concerns for the universal church over this matter?

   - How about your local church?

   - Do you feel equipped to discuss this issue with friends, family, or members of your congregation?

4. Discuss how much the answers shifted since the kickoff.

5. Point out that we each get to choose whether we want to draw people toward God or push them away. Ask for thoughts on how we can be an invitation rather than a barrier.

6. Ask what actions participants would like to take, if any, to help increase LGBTQIA+ inclusion and affirmation in the church.

7. Thank participants for their candor, thoughtfulness, and honoring of the sacred space the group has represented.

8. Close in prayer.

WHERE TO GO NEXT

Here are some things participants can do to try to increase affirmation and inclusion of LGBTQIA+ people within their congregations:

1. Ask your pastor to add quality Christian LGBTQIA+ books and resources to the church library.

2. Get involved with an organization which assists congregations in becoming welcoming, affirming, and inclusive.

    Here are a few to consider:

    - **The Reformation Project** (cross-denominational): www.reformationproject.org

    - **Q Christian Fellowship (cross-denominational)**: www.qchristian.org

    - **Reconciling Ministries Network** (began as United Methodist, but helps groups from any denomination): www.rmnetwork.org

    - **Reconciling Works** (Lutheran): www.reconcilingworks.org

    - **Dignity USA** (Catholic): www.dignityusa.org

    - **New Ways Ministry** (Catholic): www.newwaysministry.org

    - **More Light Presbyterians**: www.mlp.org

    - **Association of Welcoming and Affirming Baptists**: www.awab.org

3. Work toward including LGBTQIA+ people in the life of the church, including visible roles on Sunday mornings.

4. Consider remaining together as a group to work for continuous change and improvement.

FOR FURTHER STUDY

Below are resources for continuing your exploration of scripture and LGBTQIA+ faith.

Books and Resources about LGBTQIA+ Christian Faith

- https://www.facebook.com/WhereTrueLoveIs
- *God and the Gay Christian* by Matthew Vines.
- *Walking the Bridgeless Canyon* by Kathy Baldock.
- *Unclobber: Rethinking Our Misuse of the Bible on Homosexuality* by Colby Martin.
- *Changing Our Mind* by David Gushee.
- *Our Strangely Warmed Hearts: Coming Out into God's Call* by Bishop Karen P. Oliveto.
- *Queer Grace: An Online Encyclopedia for LGBTQ and Christian Life*: www.queergrace.com

Books about Gender-Queer Christian Faith

- *Transfigured: A 40-day journey through scripture for gender-queer and transgender people* by Suzanne DeWitt Hall.
- *Transforming: The Bible and the Lives of Transgender Christians* by Austen Hartke.
- *What Does God Think?: Transgender People and The Bible* by Cheryl Evans.

www.ingramcontent.com/pod-product-compliance
Lightning Source LLC
Chambersburg PA
CBHW081650270326
41933CB00018B/3425